BROCADE RIVER POEMS

The Lockert Library
of Poetry in Translation

For other titles in the Lockert Library
see page 109

Brocade River Poems

Selected
Works of the
Tang Dynasty
Courtesan
XUE TAO

Translated
and Introduced by
Jeanne Larsen

PRINCETON

UNIVERSITY

PRESS

Published by Princeton University Press, 41 William Street,
Princeton, New Jersey 08540

In the United Kingdom: Princeton University Press,
Guilford, Surrey
Library of Congress Cataloging in Publication Data will be
found on the last printed page of this book

ISBN 0-691-06686-8 (cloth)   0-691-01434-5 (pbk.)

The Lockert Library of Poetry in Translation is supported
by a bequest from Charles Lacy Lockert (1888-1974)

This book has been composed in Linotron Goudy. Calligraphy
on the title page is by Tang Ju-king

Clothbound editions of Princeton University Press books
are printed on acid-free paper, and binding materials are chosen
for strength and durability. Paperbacks, although satisfactory
for personal collections, are not usually suitable for
library rebinding

Printed in the United State of American by Princeton
University Press, Princeton, New Jersey

For my parents,
George Edward Larsen and
Hope Harrin Larsen

❦ CONTENTS

❧ INTRODUCTION

This book contains literary translations of about three-fourths of the surviving poems of Xue Tao (also spelled Hsüeh T'ao), a woman born at the midpoint of China's great Tang dynasty. The translations are intended for the general reader of poetry rather than for scholars, but they are grounded in careful readings of the originals. In what follows you will find a short biography, an introduction to Xue's work, and a few comments on the way the poems have been translated. The notes at the end of the book put individual poems into their social and literary contexts, point out where the translations are especially "free," indicate lost ambiguities and puns, and explain literary and historical allusions. No translation can do what the original poem does, but maybe in this new language something like the voice of that long-dead woman will ring in your mind's ear.

A LIFE OF XUE TAO

There are many fascinating stories about Xue Tao's life. No doubt some of them are true. This much is certain: she was born around A.D. 768 and evidently died late in 831 or early the next year; she had a considerable reputation as a poet in an age of great poets; and she lived as an independent woman when that was not an easy thing to do.

In part because she was a woman (and not one of the self-sacrificing "exemplary women" whose biographies were recorded in the official histories), other information about Xue's life is sketchy. Much of what can be said comes from her associations with powerful and famous men, or from knowing about what it meant to be a courtesan and a Taoist churchwoman (nüguan) during the Tang, or from gossipy anecdotes written down long after her death. The latter cannot be trusted to give us "facts," but like her poems, they tell us she was gifted, strong-minded, and intelligent—a woman who lived by her wits.

Xue Tao was one of what Virginia Woolf, writing of another place and time, called "the daughters of educated men": women of this class occasionally acquired some of what was provided by the formal education given their brothers. Her biographers tell us that Xue came from "a good family of Chang'an," the capital of the Tang empire. But her father, a minor government official, was posted to the provincial capital Chengdu, in what is now Sichuan province. It is quite possible that the family actually moved from their old home in the imperial city before her birth.

She grew up in the "Brocade City." (Chengdu took its nickname from the Brocade River, which winds around it.) It governed the Western Rivers district, half of the province of Jiannan, which was centered in the fertile, mountain-ringed Sichuan basin. The region—often called by its old name, Shu—had a long and proud tradition of poets.

During Xue's lifetime, the prosperous Western Rivers district was often nearly independent of the Tang empire's weakened central government, though most of its military governors were loyal to the throne. But life there was not always peaceful. Control of the Chengdu garrison meant de facto control of the entire district. Rebellious generals temporarily seized power shortly before Xue Tao was born, again when she was about fifteen, and a third time when she was close to forty. Moreover, Shu bordered on the lands of the Nanzhao, the Tibeto-Burman people to the south and west who were struggling with the Chinese empire for dominance in Central Asia. A few years before Xue Tao's death the Nanzhao took advantage of a corrupt district government to invade Chengdu, sacking the city and taking captives into slavery. Still, the poet lived to see a new governor rebuild defenses; she celebrates his work in her poem "For the Opening of Border Strategy Tower."

Perhaps Xue Tao's father died in, or was executed as a result of, one of those early rebellions. Whatever the cause, he was dead by the time she reached marriageable age in her mid-teens. Her widowed mother did not return to the extended family in the imperial capital, which suggests that they were not well off.

Her father may have given Xue Tao one important thing: some kind of literary education, including knowledge of how to compose poems that fit a complex musical pattern of word-pitch (the "tones" of spoken Chinese). The best-known story about her childhood tells us:

When Tao was seven or eight years old, she knew the prosody of tonally regulated verse. Her father, sitting one day in the garden, pointed to a wellside paulownia tree and said,

"A single old paulownia in the yard:
Its soaring trunk goes right into the clouds."

He ordered Tao to continue the poem. Following the tonal pattern, she said,

"Its branches welcome birds from north and south;
Leaves bid farewell to winds that come and go."

Her father was sorrowful for a long time.

Such an early display of talent in poetic composition suggests that Xue Tao was something of a child prodigy. (Imagine an American eight-year-old completing a perfect sonnet!) Of course the story may not be true; such tales of childhood genius are common in the recorded lives of Chinese literary men and women, where marking the individual as "A Poet" was more important than accuracy in factual detail.

But the last comment in the anecdote is the telling one. Even though the girl's father ordered her to complete the poem, the story paradoxically suggests a pressure toward silence, the same pressure that many Western feminist critics have seen our own culture giving women who might presume to become writers and thus enter the sphere of activities reserved for men. Why was the father unhappy? Because the poem's lone high-reaching tree whose guests, the birds and winds, never stay is a figure of the courtesan, and the child's reference to it presumably foreshadows her own fate. This, the unspoken moral seems to be, is what happens to girls who make poetry.

When this little story is placed in the context of other such anecdotes about the childhoods of female poets, the implied warning to gifted girls becomes more obvious: dare to assert your literary voice and you'll wind up breaking the heart of the father you are duty-bound to obey and please. He may associate with the glamorous and gifted women of the entertainment district, so many of whom compose poems and song lyrics, but he certainly doesn't want his daughter to become one. Another such story variously told of the young Xue and a ten-year-old girl surnamed Ji (said to have lived in Chang'an in the fourteenth century) follows the same pattern: a poem presaging life as a courtesan elicits the father's sorrow. And there is a similar tale, complete with paternal distress at the future the girl's art foretells, about the childhood of the eighth-century poet known as Li Jilan (Li Chi-lan) or Li Ye (Li Yeh).

The edifying works intended for literate women—*The Women's Classic of Filial Piety*, *The Analects for Women*, and *Biographies of Exemplary Women*—remind us of the pervasiveness of this pressure toward female silence in the Confucian tradition. Nor is the mixed fate of life as a courtesan (which did after all provide a rather special kind of status for the most fortunate) the only "bad end" used to scare off girls who would be poets. Execution for treason or for murder, ghost stories indicating a death in prison or a restless afterlife as an untrustworthy seductress: such scandalous stories about Xue, Li, and the third of the most well-known literary women of the Tang, Yu Xuanji (Yü Hsüan-chi), circulated centuries after they died.

And yet, without wealth or the status provided by a powerful father Xue Tao's chances for fulfilling the expectations for women—silent submission, chastity, an undeveloped intelligence, and economic dependence—through a "good" marriage as formal wife to an official were not very strong. But how did she come to enter the ranks of the courtesans, the polished *musiciennes* and hostesses of Chengdu's glittering entertainment district? If her father *was* executed for treason, she might have been sent to one of the houses there, a common punishment for families of criminals. It seems likely, however, that such a sensational story would have survived in some account of Xue Tao's life.

Some of the biographical sources do suggest a "wild" youth for the future courtesan. One, written in Chengdu in the late thirteenth or the fourteenth century, states:

Her mother, widowed, raised Tao. When she reached marriageable age, she became known outside [the household] for her poetry. Also, she was good at brushing her eyebrows and applying powder. This was not the way things were done in the better families. There were guests who had intimate conversations with her in secret.

This account raises three unanswerable questions. Are the "guests" simply "retainers of a high-ranking noble," or are they "clients" (the Chinese word *ke* covers both meanings), indicating unlicensed prostitution? Are the "intimate conversations" a circumlocution for sexual intimacy, or do they merely suggest coquetry? And most importantly, is the story true, or is it a retrospective justification for her eventual entry into the government's official registry of courtesans and entertainers?

Whether by choice or from lack of an alternative, Xue did enter that registry, joining a world where women were valued as conversationalists and *artistes*, where talent mattered more than beauty, where men relaxed or made political and business deals or found the womanly intellectual companionship that their wives' limited domestic education made impossible. Sex was part of it, of course, but not the greatest part.

Female entertainers in medieval China looked with contempt on the women who worked in mere "marketplace brothels." The entertainers had guilds and paid taxes to the government that regulated and protected them. In cities throughout the empire, courtesans performed at public events, and Chengdu in particular was well-known for its entertainment district. At parties or on outings to the countryside these women facilitated much of the social (and hence political and intellectual) interaction of powerful and cultured men. The leaders of society competed for their attention. After years of training in the arts, famous courtesans attached to the most prestigious houses kept suites of rooms that they decorated as they wished, in complexes with reception rooms, banquet halls, and tasteful gardens, set along lantern-lit avenues.

Those men who had enough wealth and status to associate with courtesans like Xue Tao almost certainly had one or more wives at home and probably officially recognized concubines as well. In *Sexual Life In Ancient China* Robert van Gulik points out that, given the cultural expectations that they not only produce sons but keep these women sexually satisfied, a desire for intercourse is not likely to have been most men's major motive for establishing relationships with women in the entertainment district. What they did want, and got, was intimacy with intellectual equals, flattering and flirtatious repartee, and an educated audience for the poetry that every well-bred gentleman could compose and recite.

Still, it is important not to romanticize these women's lives. Their freedom (at least in theory) to select or reject a particular lover gave them a great deal more autonomy than most women had in traditional China. But even the most fortunate of the courtesans acted out of economic necessity. And the future of the woman who did not direct her energies in one way or another to pleasing her patron or the clients of her house could not have been bright.

Xue Tao was one of the lucky ones. Governments regularly employed courtesans as hostesses for official banquets, and at some point early in Xue's adult career (perhaps even before she formally registered as a courtesan), word of her literary talent reached the new military governor, Wei Gao. He summoned her to "serve wine and compose poems." For the next twenty years Xue Tao was the protégée of this capable general and popular ruler.

Xue's works suggest that she often entertained important visitors to Chengdu by composing poems in their honor at parties or farewell feasts. With the growth of her fame as a poet and as a gifted calligrapher, the flattery of such attention must have been increasingly useful to Wei Gao in political dealings.

According to many writers, Xue Tao was awarded the title "Collator" (*jiaoshu*). This office, which provided status and income but required little work, was awarded to talented young men as a kind of "writer-in-residence" position. But women were not given such posts. Other sources tell us that Wei Gao (or possibly a powerful successor of his, Wu Yuanheng) requested that she be made a Collator, but someone in the central government refused. What seems most

xvi

likely is that although the governor's nomination was turned down, so remarkable was his gesture, and so deserving was this exceptional woman, she was ever after associated in people's minds with the office she might have held. She is often referred to not as "Collator" but by the unofficial title "Collatrix" (*nüjiaoshu*).

Xue Tao's reputation spread in other ways. Tales of her intelligence and wit were passed around in the entertainment district of the imperial capital itself. The tenth-century work "Talented Women of Shu" tells us:

Xue's talents were outstanding. When it came to banter, she had immediate comebacks. The ordinary run of courtesans attached to military governments didn't measure up to the Collator. . . . Her poems were circulated in the four directions. . . . When imperial emissaries arrived in Shu, a great many of them would ask to meet Xue.

There are several widely circulated stories of her topping the efforts of important government figures in literary party games, to the amusement of the other guests. One such quick improvisation—a clever bit of writing by Xue on the subject of calligraphy—may have marked the start of her relationship with the romantic literary genius and statesman Yuan Zhen (Yuan Chen). In any case, they somehow became friends and, it seems, lovers.

Yuan is one of the most interesting figures of his time. He is known for his poetry, his prose, his influence on the literary movements of the era, and the rapid ups and downs of his political career. He rose to the level of prime minister, but he was banished more than once. It seems almost inevitable that the name of a man popularly considered both brilliant and given to transient love affairs would be linked romantically with Xue's. But though the reality may (or may not) have been embroidered, the two did exchange poems. The last poem in this collection, "Sending Old Poems to Yuan Zhen," suggests that Xue—who was probably in her early forties when Yuan, then thirty, visited her region in 809—acted as a literary mentor to the younger poet. Its tone reveals a bantering but caring relationship.

Just who introduced the two poets, and whether Xue Tao might have left Chengdu to live for a time with Yuan, is unclear. Legends and possibilities for speculation abound. Central to them is Xue's famous poem sequence "Ten Partings." The poems, with their many witty puns on erotic terms, indicate that they were written for a lover, an important man who sent the poet away after a falling out. Yuan was in Shu for less than a year, but something must be made of the suggestion, in three of the poems, of a relationship of four or five years before the quarrel. Is this evidence that Xue *did* live with him elsewhere, or simply that they had corresponded for some years before meeting?

Or were the poems written for someone else? While many sources say the addressee was Yuan, others say it was Wei Gao. The poem "Parrot Parted from Her Cage," which suggests the speaker's banishment to the desert wilderness of the northwest frontier, fits the latter theory better. Still, whatever happened, Xue Tao was capable of getting herself back home to Chengdu.

Her poems were important in developing and maintaining her social and intellectual relationships in other ways as well. Poem exchanges played an important role in the literary and emotional lives of the educated in medieval China. Most men of culture worked for the government and were frequently transferred to distant posts; they were often separated from their friends for years and corresponded at least partly in verse. Poets would respond to poems they had been sent by returning another on the same theme, sometimes using the same rhyme, or even the very rhyme words of the original poem itself. And groups of people at banquets or on excursions composed poems on the occasion, often to a specified rhyme.

Over half of Xue Tao's extant works are addressed to some individual. As she rose from clever entertainer to well-known poet, Xue began to receive poems from people who knew her only by reputation. One source tells us that twenty-eight "famous lords" competed in exchanging rhyming poems with her; it names eleven of the most powerful and talented men of the age, poets who wrote in a wide range of styles and themes. Some of them had lived in, or had reason to visit, Chengdu. But others were, at most, friends of friends.

Most of the poems she received in these exchanges are lost. A few examples, however, remain: Yuan Zhen's "Sent to be Presented to Xue Tao"; Bo Juyi's "Presented to Xue Tao"; and another poem variously attributed to Wang Jian or Hu Ceng, though the latter would probably have written it as a posthumous tribute.* To produce poems for such accomplished poet-officials, Xue must have possessed both confidence and considerable versatility, as her works show.

In addition to these literary friendships Xue maintained relationships with the military governors in Chengdu throughout her adult life. Even after she retired from her position as an official hostess, sometime in her early forties, Xue's reputation as a poet ensured that she would retain status and respect in the provincial capital.

In moving to her country place on the banks of the Brocade River, just south of the city wall, Xue Tao did what only the most fortunate of retired courtesans were able to do: she lived independently. It was more usual to leave the entertainment quarter by marrying a merchant or other commoner, or by becoming the concubine or the "household entertainer" of an official. Other women fell, with age, to lower status work as prostitutes. A few managed to open their own establishments, while still others entered Buddhist or Taoist convents.

Xue's country home was a pleasant one. A generation earlier the most highly regarded of all Chinese poets, Du Fu (Tu Fu), had built his own retreat not far away. Some of his poems depict the pastoral beauty and meditative peace of the area. They also remind us of the attractive force of the "poet-recluse" role in the lives of Chinese literary men—and point up Xue's exceptional success in claiming that role as a woman in a strongly patriarchal culture.

Today in Chengdu there is a riverside park downstream from the area Xue retired to. It contains a "Xue Tao Well" and a "River Gazing Tower" popularly associated with the poet. There are also several smaller buildings, including one named after Xue's final residence, the "Poem Chanting Tower," which just might have stood on or near this site.

---

* Some readers will know the last three poets under the alternate spellings of Po Chü-i, Wang Chien, and Hu Ts'eng.

The well's water evokes the beautiful handmade paper that became an important part of the Xue Tao legend. Paper making was a highly developed art form in Tang times, and poets prized attractive paper on which they might brush their words. One source says Xue made special "Xue Tao Slips" in ten colors, which was the custom of nearby paper makers, but others tell us the paper was a deep crimson, the color associated with poem exchanges between courtesans and their admirers. Another tradition has it that she made a kind of paper known as "Pineflower Slips"; this name, in a different rendition, became the title of Florence Ayscough and Amy Lowell's 1921 anthology of translated Chinese poems, *Fir-Flower Tablets*. Whatever the color, her chief innovation (which the historical sources make much of) was to make the paper in smaller sheets, suited for brief poems.

"In her twilight years," according to many biographers, Xue "withdrew from the world to live in seclusion at Rinseflowers Stream [another name for the Brocade River], and wore the habit of a Taoist churchwoman." Such a move does not necessarily indicate a life of solitude or pure religious devotion. Rather, it fits the pattern of reclusion often found in the stylized biographies of Chinese poets. Xue Tao certainly still received visitors; indeed, her home at Rinseflowers Stream might have resembled, at times, a literary salon.

Nor do the many scandalous tales of sexual depravity in Taoist convents (partly fostered by Buddhist rivals, partly by the Taoist popular tradition of promoting good health and longevity through special sexual techniques, and partly by the genuine corruption in some Taoist retreats) mean that we should see Xue Tao's life as a *nüguan* as in any way immoral. To wear the cap of a woman of the Tao may well have been something like what entering a Christian convent was for some intellectual upper-class women of medieval Europe: the assertion of a certain independence (at least in daily life) from a male-dominated society and a gesture of dedication to the life of the mind. Nineteen Tang royal princesses (as well as a great many former palace ladies and retired courtesans) became *nüguan*. A few poems by some of them still survive, a reminder that although today we have many more poems by Xue Tao than by any other Tang dynasty woman she was in fact part of a long and continuing female tradition in Chinese poetry.

THE POEMS

The title of this selection of Xue Tao's work echoes that of her *Brocade River Collection*, which was lost sometime after the year 1304. All told, ninety poems attributed to her by one source or another still exist, though two or three of these may have been written by someone else.* Since the poems circulated in hand-copied manuscripts before they were finally printed, there are a number of textual variants, most of which are noted in the Chinese texts from the *Complete Tang Poems* included in this book. Knowing which version is "correct" is impossible, so I have followed the text that seems to yield the best English poem.

The sad thing is that there were once about five times as many of Xue's poems in circulation. It is difficult to say whether the extant ones are typical of the full range of her work, since those that fit the conventional image of a love-lorn poetess or those that pun amusingly on amatory language may have had a better chance of surviving. Still, the variety of what remains is impressive.

The group selected for translation here is not quite representative either. It neglects Xue Tao's many adept poems of praise for powerful men. While such encomia were a standard part of the repertoire of Tang writers (and, for example, of such English poets as Sidney, John Davies, Ben Jonson, Marvell, and Dryden), they seem likely to strike the contemporary Western reader as sycophantic, however skillfully done.† Other poems were left out because, though they might be good examples of their genre, they depended heavily on the conventions of medieval Chinese poetry or turned chiefly on literary or historical allusions.

* Another poem is said to have been recited by Xue's ghost to a young man imprisoned in Chengdu. There is some chance, of course, that this poem really was her work incorporated into a story; however, other verses—attributed to her seductive ghost in a Ming dynasty tale—are almost certainly apocryphal.
† "Lyric Sent to a Taoist Recluse," here included among other poems on religious themes, will give you an idea of what Xue's praise poems are like.

Readers may find more about the allusions, the place of certain poems in the tradition of Chinese verse on the same topic, the details of the many mysteries in Xue Tao's biography, my sources of information, and the *literal* readings of all the original poems in my doctoral thesis, *The Chinese Poet Xue Tao: The Life and Works of a Mid-Tang Woman.* * The versions here follow the same order; they are grouped by genre or subject matter: allegorical *yongwu* poems are followed by parting poems, poems on love and on courtesans, occasional verse, poems of protest and banishment, those on religious themes, a group on human beings in the natural world, and a few poems to other poets that touch on the subjects of writing and poetics.

Clearly, Xue Tao wrote in a multitude of literary voices and stances. Her *yongwu* poems (the name means "singing of objects" in Chinese) celebrate things from the natural world while exploring their allegorical significance in her literary heritage. Some are delightful riddles; others skillfully combine an appreciation in sensuous detail of the bamboo or peony or cicada with a didactic or self-expressive message. The poem "Cicadas" in particular shows in its unpolished diction and use of traditional Confucian allegory the concerns of the Tang *fugu* ("restore antiquity") movement of moral poetry.

Xue's parting poems range from the formal to the familiar while observing the decorums of other Tang dynasty poems of farewell. Life for government officials and their associates was marked by frequent separations from friends and acquaintances, often for life. This reality, and the attention given to proper and polite observance of formalities in Xue Tao's world, meant that the occasion of parting was an important one. The intensity of emotion in her poems written for someone's departure varies with the degree of intimacy between poet and recipient; the three chosen for this collection are among the more personal. But even those that are evidently obligatory poems produced at state farewell banquets provided her an opportunity for artful and pleasing literary expression.

* University of Iowa, 1983.

Poems by Xue Tao on love and related subjects range from the rather ascetic rejection of sensual pleasure in the first poem of this collection, through her exploration of melancholy desire in the "Gazing at Spring" cycle, to the cheerfully erotic. In each mood she is successful in moving the reader to a responsive sorrow or to delight. Similarly, her poems depicting courtesans range from the witty derision of "Willow Floss" to the suppressed sadness surrounding the courtesanlike flowering trees in "Mountain Pear Blossoms."

Contemporary Western readers, influenced by the high value we set on spontaneity and originality, must remember that neither of these qualities is necessarily eliminated by Xue's creative variations on the rich store of set structures and images from her literary heritage. Her verse on various social occasions shows especially well that she had both artistic skills and literary sophistication comparable to those of the best poets of the Mid-Tang, the silver age in which she lived. Her banquet poems describe the splendor of the scene, praise the host, and use as closure particularly effective versions of the conventional expression of regret that such great pleasure must end. The two on the Mid-Autumn Festival employ the rich associations of that holiday to make her own unique statements, one elevated, one cleverly suggestive. And her "thank-you" poems—along with an apology for missing an outing—confirm the reader's sense of Xue's control of her craft.

Among the most striking of Xue Tao's works are those on the subjects of war and banishment. The two "For Someone Far Away" protest the effects on women's lives of their men's absence at the front. Those that seem to be written after her own banishment to the northwest frontier subtly apply evocative features of a popular lyrical topic. Despite the frustrating losses in translation, patient readers of the "Ten Partings" sequence should come to understand just why their titillating wordplay, mock humility, and sheer rhetorical power won such popularity.

Xue's various poems on holy sites and holy persons remind us of the flourishing of Buddhism, Taoism, and folk religion in her time. As with many of her peers, it is difficult to know how much these poems reflect true devotion and how much they simply express the widespread contemporary taste for religious themes and imagery. Yet in either case, her delicate, penetrating descriptions of a monk's music and the scenes at shrines or temples call for powerful responses, whether spiritual or aesthetic. And, like her eventual retirement as a *nüguan*, a number of Xue's poems suggest the value of withdrawal to a life of spiritual peace.

Chinese nature poetry is, for good reason, the most popular with many Western readers. Xue Tao's poems tend to focus not on the sublimity of the wild but on human activity—boating parties and mountain outings—or on scenes like artificial ponds, orchards, and the view from atop a tower. Many of the poems explore the meaning of the natural world for human beings: what she shows us variously sustains exhilaration, longing, awe, military preparedness, and the life of the imagination.

The last four poems in this collection seem to manifest something of Xue's views on poetry itself. All of them appear to have been occasioned either by an exchange of poems or a letter of high literary quality; perhaps this intertextual dialogue stimulated her critical sense. In the poem for Lord Commissioner Wen the ethically oriented *fugu* poetics appears in her use of past glories as the standard of evaluation for the present, though the poem's possible hint of flirtatiousness certainly counters the austere (and arguably misogynist) values of that movement to "restore antiquity." Xue's praise for the creative skill of Licentiate Zhu resembles more extreme examples of one strain of Chinese poetics because of the great scope and high value she assigns to Zhu's imagination; at the same time the poem is also reminiscent of traditional theorists who stressed mastery of poetic craft. In writing for Grand Secretary Du and for Yuan Zhen, Xue exemplifies the importance of older poets as mentors to younger ones and of poetry as an instrument of social intercourse for Tang intellectuals. The latter poem also implies a "self-expressive" theory of lyric poetry.

An early twelfth-century annotation in the *Xuanhe shupu*, a catalogue of calligraphic works held in the imperial treasury, provides a typical assessment of Xue Tao's talents:

xxiv

Although Tao lost her chastity and was lowly [in social rank], she had a re-fined manner. Thus, whenever her literary works came out, people passed them around eagerly and took pleasure in them. She wrote characters with-out the air of a woman; the power of her pen was strict and strong. Her "run-ning script" style had wonderful places rather in the style of [the famous] Wang Xizhi. Had she had a bit more learning, she would have been a [great calligrapher like] Lady Wei. She always loved to write out her own poems. Her language was skillful and the ramifications of her thought stood unri-valed. As for her polite responses to others' writing, and her witty epigrams, it was because of these that she acquired a reputation.

This passage reveals a pattern seen in almost every critical response to Xue Tao's work, Western or Japanese, traditional or modern Chinese. Her life and poems are understood always in light of her gender. Since the poet and her readers have lived and worked in cul-tures where male-claimed modes of literary and intellectual operation are taken as the norm, how could it be otherwise? But sometimes peo-ple seem to have been blinded to other qualities of the writer and her work: the poet is read as "poetess," and much of the complexity of her texts may be overlooked.

Xue Tao had a rich heritage of poems by women to draw upon, some by the wives and daughters of the elite, and some by working women, including anonymous peasants, boatwomen, and nightclub singers. The one female poet that a Westerner starting to read Chinese poetry is likely to hear of, Li Qingzhao (Li Ch'ing-chao), lived some three centuries after Xue. But the definitive anthology of Tang poetry, the *Complete Tang Poems*, contains nearly six hundred poems attributed to about 130 women—out of a total of approxi-mately 2,250 poets. There are also many women from before the Tang era for whom a few poems and a scattering of biographical details survive. Men, too, had long written poems in the persona of a lan-guishing, sensual palace lady, or in the more colloquial voice of a *chanteuse* like the famous Ziye (Tzu-yeh or "Midnight"), thus provid-ing additional models of poems with female speakers. Xue used such traditions when it was appropriate, but she did not limit herself to them.

Xue's knowledgable use of Tang conventions of voice, content, and tone in poems on a wide range of subjects marks her as a self-aware, articulate member of that great literary community. The qualities of theme and craft that her poems have in common with the best of the Mid-Tang era indicate what too many of her critics have been unwilling or unable to perceive. Though her life and her art were shaped by her gender, the cramped quarters assigned to women did not suffice. The depth of thought, emotional range, and aesthetic control in her work mark her as a versatile and compelling poet. And they speak to us today.

THE TRANSLATION

My translations are meant to be literary ones, as faithful to the originals as my goal of lively and euphonious English will allow. Individual lines of the original Chinese are rendered as brief stanzas; the fundamental order of presentation has not been changed, but the arrangement of words *within* the Chinese line has been altered freely. Normal, effective English word order took precedence over mimicry of Chinese syntax or grammatical function. As a result, Xue's skillful creation of parallel couplets has been blurred over in places. But like the rhyme of the originals, such parallelism is a rhetorical device that, while quite appealing in its own right, may distance the poems from the contemporary American ear.

Some translators of Chinese poetry abhor any insertion of words natural to English but often not found in the compressed, even stylized, language that is literary Chinese: no "thes," few prepositions and few "ands," "whens," and "buts" appear in the original texts. The problem is that what English expresses through the use of such words is in fact often quite clearly present in other ways for the reader of literary Chinese, who knows (for example) that the first line of a couplet is often subordinate grammatically to the second and who mentally fills in a "while" or the like, as needed. When choices were necessary, I often suggested one possible way of filling in rather than making the kind of telegraphic renditions that are pleasantly exotic but in their own way untrue to the *effect* of the original words. This means, however, that some nice ambiguities have been lost.

A similar problem arises with the much-discussed freedom of literary Chinese from distinctions between singular and plural (unless they are desired), from verb tense, and even from explicitly stated subjects for some sentences. In the hands of a Du Fu or a Wang Wei these linguistic resources can be manipulated with breath-taking results. But for many Chinese poems, most of Xue Tao's among them, it seems more "faithful" to the experience of reading the original to look at its context and select an unobtrusive option. Often this context is signaled by the title: a parting poem might just as well be spoken by "I" to "you," though the more distanced "she" and "he" would also do.

A few explanatory words have been added to some of the allusions in Xue's poems. Other allusions have been replaced by a more familiar phrase (for example, "Shangri-La" for "Wuling"). The notes at the end of the book provide background information, but they are no more than a supplement to poems that should stand alone. I have taken advantage of the traditional Chinese editor's freedom to alter titles in order to provide more information about some of the poems.

The best way to appreciate fully the beauty of Xue Tao's poems is still to read the originals. Translators have to make choices where no choice is really right. They know, perhaps better than anyone, how often they have failed. But they also feel their debts: to earlier translators who introduced them to new literatures, to those who helped them learn to read the poems they try to re-create, and to whatever poet spoke to them so strongly that they were willing to attempt what they knew could not, really, be done.

BROCADE RIVER POEMS

YONGWU POEMS

Poem in Answer to Someone's "After the Rains, Taking Pleasure among the Bamboo"

When the spring
rains come
to the southern sky

you can just make out—how
odd!—the look of frost,
the cool allure of snow.

The mass of plants
mingle thick,
indiscriminant, and lush.

But this one
with her empty heart
can hold herself alone.

Her groves kept the seven sages
high on poetry and wine.

Yet earlier still, her
tear-splotched leaves
grieved with Lord Shun's wives.

When your year turns to winter, sir,
you will know her worth—

her ice-gray green,
her virtue:
rare, strong nodes.

酬人雨後玩竹

南天春雨時。那墮雪霜姿。眾類亦云茂。虛心能自持。多留嵇阮醉。早伴舜妃悲。

晚歲一作歲晚君能賞。蒼蒼勁節奇。

3

Cicadas

Dew-rinsed:
their pure notes
carry far.

Windblown:
as dry, fasting leaves
are blown.

Chirr after chirr,
as if in unison.

But each perches
on its one branch,
alone.

蟬 一作聞蟬

露滌清音遠。風吹數一作散葉齊。聲聲似相接。各在一枝棲。

獵蕙微風遠。飄弦噪一聲。林梢鳴淅瀝。松徑夜凄清。

風

Wind

Seeking marsh
orchids, a light
zephyr ranges.

It wafts over strings;
they cry out,
one chord.

Twigs in the woods
sing in whistles and rustles.

Along paths through the pine trees:
night-bracing,
fresh.

月

魄依鉤樣小。扇逐漢機圓。細影將圓質。人間幾處看。

Moon

Its nascent crescent spirit
takes a hook-shape,
small.

Then, a fan
from the Han loom,
round.

Sliver of shine:
its nature, to wax full.

Where on earth
can such a thing
be seen?

Peonies

Last spring they fell and
scattered, when the
late spring came.

Drops wet
crimson slips—
resenting separation.

Constantly brooding:
will we drift apart
like the Witch Gorge lovers?

How could it happen,
to come together
twice in Shangri-La?

It's always like this.
I catch their scent and
old feelings come around.

Wordless:
still, we know one another,
or should.

All I want
is to take my quilts,
spread them beside the porch rail,

and deep in the night,
at ease together,
speak of longing, of love.

牡丹

去春零落暮春時。淚溼紅箋怨別離。常恐便同巫峽散。因何重有武陵期。傳情每向馨香得。

不語還應彼此知。只欲欄邊安枕席。夜深閒共說相思。

7

和劉賓客玉蕣

瓊枝的皪露珊珊。欲折如拔玉一作霞彩寒。閒拂朱房何所似。緣山偏映月一作日輪殘。

Poem Rhyming with Liu Yuxi's "Jade Rose of Sharon"

Stalks jewel-vivid
where dew glitters.

You want to pick one:
it seems to open,
jade-bright, cool.

Idly, stroke
the crimson chamber:
what place
is its like?

On green hills the
slanting glow
as the moon's disk wanes.

🌿 FAREWELL POEMS

Seeing-Off a Friend

River country:
reeds and rushes
decked with frost at night.

The moon's chill light,
the hills'
glazed green,
go dusky and blur together.

Who can say,
after tonight
a thousand miles apart?

Distant dreams of a traveler
go as far
as the border is long.

送友人

水國蒹葭夜有霜。月寒山色共蒼蒼。誰言千里自今夕。離夢杳如關塞一作路長。

Seeing-Off Associate Secretary Yao

Early fall and the river willows'
thousand-stranded withes

bend down lithe,
wave up in the wind,
their color
not yet gone.

"Willow" means "stay":
I'll break one off
for your farewell gift.

Do not let this
moonlit haze
know the sorrow of
two towns.

送姚員外

萬條江柳早秋枝。裊地翻風色未衰。欲折爾來將贈別。莫敎煙月兩鄉悲。

Seeing-Off Zheng, Prefect of Meizhou

Rain darkens Mothbrow Mountain;
the river waters flow.

Parting:
her face behind her sleeves, she
stands atop the watchtower.

Two matched pennons,
a thousand mounts
in pairs on the Eastern Road—

alone, she gazes
like a faithful
wife toward the column's head.

送鄭眉 一作資州

雨暗眉山江水流。離人掩袂立高樓。雙旌千騎駢東陌。獨有羅敷望上頭。

13

✿ POEMS ON LOVE AND ON COURTESANS

春望 一作望春詞四首

花開不同賞。花落不同悲。欲問相思處。花開花落時。

Gazing at Spring, I

Flowers bloom:
no one
to enjoy them with.

Flowers fall:
no one
with whom to grieve.

I wonder when love's
longings
stir us most—

when flowers bloom,
or when flowers fall?

揽草結同心。將以遺知音。春愁正斷絕。春鳥復哀吟。
一作蘹

Gazing at Spring, II

I gather herbs
and tie
a lover's knot

to send to one
who understands my songs.

So now I've cut
that springtime sorrow
off.

And now the spring-struck birds
renew their cries.

18

風花日將老。佳期猶渺渺。不結同心人。空結同心草。

Gazing at Spring, III

Windblown flowers
grow older day by day.

And our best season
dwindles in the past.

Without someone
to tie the knot
of love,

no use to tie up
all those love-knot herbs.

那堪花滿枝。翻作兩相思。玉筯垂朝鏡。春風知不知。

Gazing at Spring, IV

How can I bear it?
Blossoms fill the branch,

stirring coupled
thoughts.

Jade-white tears
in two lines hang
down my morning mirror:

does the spring wind know
or does it not?

峨嵋山下水如油。憐我心同不繫舟。何日片帆離錦浦。櫂聲齊唱發中流。

鄉思

Homethoughts

At the foot of Mothbrow Mountain,
the river:
glossy, slick.

It grieves me
that our two hearts match
and yet your boat's not moored.

When will a slip of sail
leave the Brocade City's banks,

as we sing together
to the sound of oars
and set out
in midstream?

秋泉

冷色初澄一帶煙。幽聲遙瀉十絲弦。長來枕上牽情_{一作愁思}。不使愁人半夜眠。

Autumn, Hearing the Headwaters on a Moonlit Night

When that chilly hue strikes clear
the single strand of mist,

a muffled trill slides
far away:
ten silken strings.

It comes, long-drawn, to pillows.
It tugs at hearts and thoughts.

It will not let
at midnight
those who sorrow sleep.

Riverbank

Pair by pair—and
suddenly!—west winds
blow wild geese back.

But human bodies,
human hearts,
go down on their own.

If not for these secret love notes,
each word a talisman,

who could stand
in dream
after dream
beside the River Clear?

江邊

西風忽報雁一作燕雙雙。人世心形兩自降。不爲魚腸有眞訣。誰能夢夢一作夜夜立淸江。

Willow Floss

柳絮

二月楊花輕復微。春風搖蕩惹人衣。他家本是無情物。一任一作向南飛又北飛。

Early March: willow catkins
light and fancy-free.

The spring breeze makes them weave
and waver
and tease at people's clothes.

The girls in that house?
They are, at root,
unfeeling things.

Once committed to flying south,
they're off and flying—
north.

棠梨花和李太尉

吳均蕙圃移嘉木。正及東溪春雨時。日晚鶯啼何所爲。淺深紅膩壓繁枝。

Mountain Pear Blossoms: Poem Rhyming with One by Li, General of the Armies

This fragrant garden:
like Wu Jun, that gifted man,
you've brought in lovely trees.

They come right up to the eastern brook
in the season of spring rains.

As day grows late
the warblers cry,
for what?
for sake of what?

Rouge pink and lipstick red,
the blossoms
weigh down luxurious limbs.

❦ OCCASIONAL VERSE

Banquet Poem for Minister Wu Yuanheng, Governor of the Western Rivers District

The setting sun on thick town walls
where evening fog gathers,

tortoise-shell mats on carved tables:
all arranged
for the nobles' feast.

Since you have ordered the blazing moon
to be our courtyard fire,

we won't let the pearl-sewn shades
be lowered
past that jade-white hook.

上川主武元衡相國二首 一本無元衡二字

落日重城夕霧收。玳筵雕俎薦諸侯。因令朗月當庭燎。不使珠簾下玉鉤。

東閣移尊綺席陳。貂簪龍節更宜春。軍城畫角三聲歇。雲幕初垂紅燭新。

Another Banquet Poem for Minister Wu

Goblets and embroidered mats
set out in the east pavillion,

guests with dragon badges,
guests in sable hair clasps:
right for seeing-in
the spring.

When the painted horn from the army camp
has wailed three times,
and stopped,

the misty blinds are lowered at last,
and red candles
lighted anew.

Rained-Out on the Mid-Autumn Festival, I

Alarming gusts come a thousand miles.
This northern wind cuts deep.

The riverside city is desolate:
all day,
cloud on cloud.

Who is sorry
that we can't make
the usual holiday climb?

Better to pity chrysanthemums'
wintry scent,
and their showy hues
gone gold.

九日遇雨二首

萬里驚飆朔氣深。江城蕭索晝陰陰。誰憐不得登山去。可惜褒芳色似金。

茱萸秋節佳期阻。金菊寒花滿院香。神女欲來知有意。先令雲雨暗池塘。

Rained-Out on the Mid-Autumn Festival, II

We've dogwood for the festival
but our good time's
blocked off.

Gold-toned winter blooms:
cold fragrance fills the yard.

You know when the water nymph
is about to come;

she darkens all the ponds and pools
and orders,
yes, "clouds and rain."

A Wandering Tour of the Countryside in Spring: Sent to Master Sun

Head bent, I stood long
before a rambling rose,

lovely as fragrant basil:
its scent clung to my skirts.

Master Sun of Jadegreen Stream,
explain it all to me—

those shrikes
departing for the east,
those swallows, flying west.

春郊遊眺寄孫處士二首

低頭久立向一作白薔薇。愛似零陵香惹衣。何事碧溪一作雞孫處士。百勞東去燕西飛。

今朝縱目玩一作悅芳菲。夾纈籠裙繡地衣。滿袖滿頭兼手把。教人識是看花歸。

Another Poem for Master Sun

This morning, eyes
let free, we reveled
in those sweet smells:

blossom-print cloth surrounding skirts;
blossom-stitched mats for rest.

Filling my sleeves,
covering my head,
a fistful in each hand:

people knew that I had come
home from viewing flowers.

Sent upon Being Ill and Unable to Accompany Minister Duan on an Excursion to Wudan Temple

Wasted away: no longer
fit for audience with milord.

No use for falling flowers
to resent east winds
that bring them down.

Though I still say my heart
holds the green of spring,

what shame if my hair were reflected
in "Stone Mirror" on Wudan Hill,
bedraggled as tumbleweed!

段相國遊武擔寺病不能從題寄

消瘦翻堪見令公。落花無那恨東風。儂心猶道青春在。羞看飛蓬石鏡中。

酬雍秀才貽巴峽圖

千疊雲峯萬頃湖。白波分去遶荊吳。感君識我枕流意。重示瞿塘峽口圖。

Written to Thank Licentiate Yong for a Painting of the Yangzi Gorges

A thousand folds of
cloudy peaks
and the million-acre lake:

white waves part, depart
to swirl round the valley lands.

You knew what I want—
a hermit's life,
sleeping beside clear streams—

and gave me this scene,
the mouth of the gorge,
the river pouring through.

Written to Thank Auxiliary Xin for a Spray of Flowers

A magic blue-black bird flies east
just when plum blossoms fall.

Beak filled with flowers, it lands
on a terrace of moon-bright jade.

Like a branch from the heavenly
Kunlun range,
your gift shows true courtesy.

Holding it, I face the wind.
The blooms open
one by one.

酬辛員外折花見遺

青鳥東飛正落梅。銜花滿口下瑤臺。一枝爲授殷勤意。把向風前旋旋開。

Trying on New-Made Clothes, I

In your astral palace, I
am bestowed with scarlet silks

hazy as spirit mists
far beyond the sea.

Cool fur from the frosty moon-hare,
pure thread
of the ice-silk moth:

the Moon Lady smiles
and points
toward the Weaver Woman Star.

試新服裁製初成三首

紫陽宮裏賜紅綃。仙霧朦朧隔海遙。霜兔毳寒冰繭淨。嫦娥笑指織星橋。

38

九氣分爲九色霞。五靈仙馭五雲車。春風因過東君舍。偷樣人間染百花。

Trying on New-Made Clothes, II

The Nine Humors split and woven
into nine-colored clouds of dawn,

the Five Magic Beasts reined in
to pull
a five-cloud chariot:

east winds blowing past
the palace of Spring's Lord

stole these designs for
human realms
to dye a hundred flowers.

長裾一作裙本是上清儀。曾逐羣仙把玉芝。每到宮中歌舞會。折腰齊唱步虛詞。

Trying on New-Made Clothes, III

This skirt's in the style
worn in paradise.

It once trailed heavenly
courtiers grasping
magic-mushroom scepters.

Each time they meet at the palace,
come to sing and dance,

they bow from the waist
and chorus, "Step
through the Sky," a star-walker's song.

POEMS OF PROTEST, POEMS OF BANISHMENT

For Someone Far Away, I

Again, the his-face-flowers fall—
autumn in Sichuan's hills.

A lover's letter:
open it, find
only sorrow.

In the women's quarters
we know nothing
of things like weapons and mounts.

When the moon is high, I climb again
to the widow's walk, and watch.

贈遠二首

芙蓉新落蜀山秋。錦字開緘到是愁。閨閣不知戎馬事。月高還上望夫樓。

43

擾弱新蒲葉一作楼又齊。春深花落塞前溪。知君未轉秦關騎。月照千門掩袖啼。

For Someone Far Away, II

Flexible, frail,
new willow leaves
once more in even ranks.

Deep in spring, catkins
falling
clog
the tree-lined creek.

I know that you still guard
Qin Pass in the far northwest.

Moonlight shines on a thousand doors:
I hide my face in
my arms.

44

On Being Banished to the Borderlands: Submitted to Commander Wei

I'd heard of the hardships
in walled-off frontier towns.

But now at last
I've come to understand.

Ashamed, I take up
a song from your court

and sing it
for back-country boys.

罰赴邊有懷上韋令公二首 一作陳情上韋令公。又作上元相公。

聞道 一作說 邊城苦。今來 一作而今 到始知。羞將門下曲。唱與隴頭兒。

45

Another Poem for Commander Wei on Being Banished

黠虜一作賊貓遺命。烽煙直北愁。卻教嚴譴妾。不敢向松州。

Tibetan dogs!
They defy the emperor's rule.

Signal smoke gives rise
to a northern sorrow.

I'm chastened.
You have taught me

not to dare
face the road home from Songzhou.

46

On Arriving at the Borderlands: Submitted to Minister Wu

A firefly stays
in the weeds of the steppes.
The moon stays in the sky.

How could the firefly reach
even the border
of the moon's disk?

Their redoubled light
should shine a million miles.

But vision fails,
cut off by clouds:
honest letters don't get through.

罰赴邊上武相公二首

螢在荒蕪月在天。螢飛豈到月輪邊。重光萬里應相照。目斷雲霄信不傳。

47

按轡嶺頭寒復寒。微風細雨徹心肝。但得放兒歸舍去。山水屏風永不看。

Another Poem for Minister Wu on Arriving at the Borderlands

Pull up!
At Pull-the-Reins-Up Ridge:
cold, and colder still.

The fine drizzle, the gentle breezes
pierce
my liver and heart.

Just let me go back
to my place in town;

I swear I'll never even look
at landscapes
painted on screens.

48

❧ TEN PARTINGS

Dog Parted from Her Master

Yes, she's a good dog,
lived four or five years
within his crimson gates,

fur sweet-smelling,
feet quite clean,
master, affectionate.

Then by chance she
took a nip
and bit a well-loved guest.

Now she no longer sleeps
upon his red silk rugs.

犬離主

剔損朱門四五年。毛香足淨主人憐。無端一作只因咬著親情客一作情親爾。不得紅絲毯上眠。

需因離學今鄉往子 親留相公獅子去席。故云。

Writing Brush Parted from the Hand

Shaft
from Viet, fine hairs
from Xuan: it used to suit
his moods.

It scattered
garnets and petals
over scarlet poem-paper slips.

And then, long-used,
its rapier tip
wore out.

Now calligrapher Wang
no longer takes
it in his hand.

筆離手

越管宣毫始稱情。紅箋紙上撒一作散花瓊。都緣用久鋒頭盡。不得羲之手裏擎。

Horse Parted from Her Stable

Snow-white ears, chestnut coat,
hooves pale cobalt gray:

she chased the wind
and ran
east and west of the sun.

When she shied,
young master jadeface
tumbled down.

Now she can't cry out
one more time
between the chariot shafts.

馬離廐

雪耳紅毛淺碧蹄。追風曾到日東西。為驚玉貌郎君墜。不得華軒更一嘶。

鸚鵡離籠

隴西獨自一孤身。飛去飛來上錦茵。都緣出語無方便。不得籠中再喚人。

Parrot Parted from Her Cage

A single figure
alone in the desert wastes:

she flew, departing,
and, flying, came
to ascend the brocade seat.

Then all because she blurted
something indiscreet,

she no longer calls out
for him
from her deserted cage.

燕離巢

出入朱門未忍拋。主人常愛語交交。銜泥穢污一作汙卻珊瑚枕一作簟。不得梁間更壘巢。

Swallow Parted from Her Nest

In and out through crimson gates:
she never was put off.

Her master always loving,
she twittered
mate-sweet-mate.

But a beakful of mud
stained the coral pillow

and she no longer builds
her nest
up among his rafters.

珠離掌

皎潔圓明內外通。清光似照水晶宮。只一作都緣一點玷一作瑕相穢。不得終宵一作朝在掌中。

Pearl Parted from the Palm

White as the moon,
round, bright,
translucent to the core.

Its brilliance seems reflected
from the crystal lunar keep.

Just one fleck:
now it's defiled

and no longer spends the nights
held within his
palm.

Fish Parted from the Pond

魚離池

跳一作戲躍深一作蓮池四五秋。常搖朱尾弄綸一作銀鉤。無端擺斷芙蓉朵。不得清波更一遊。

She lept and danced in a deep
lovely pool
through four or five years' falls.

She flicked her ruddy tail
to tease
the silky line,
the hook.

Then by chance she squirmed and broke
a his-face-lily bud,

and where that water ripples clear
no longer takes
her sport.

鷹離鞲

爪利如鋒眼似鈴。平原捉兔稱高情。無端竄向青雲外。不得君王臂上一作手裏擎。

Falcon Parted from the Gauntlet

Vision keen as bell-ring,
talons, sword-tip sharp:

she seized hares, out on the plains,
and pleased his
high-flying will.

She bolted, by chance, beyond
that noble,
lofty cloud.

Now she no longer perches
on the forearm of her lord.

竹籬亭

竹籬亭

蓊鬱新栽四五行。常將勁節負秋霜。爲緣春筍鑽牆破。不得垂陰覆玉堂。

Bamboo Parted from the Pavillion

Thick and lush, new-planted
in four or five rows:

supple, constant,
sectioned stalks
bore the autumn frosts.

Since springtime shoots,
thrusting,
broke down
the wall above,

no longer may that dangling shadow
cover her
jade-white bower.

59

Mirror Parted from Its Stand

Yellow, molten gold
cast into a disk:
at first the mirror gleamed—

new crescent
turned to the fifteenth night,
a hovering full moon.

Yet concealed by countless dustmotes
it no longer mounts

within her flowery hall
its stand, that
ledge of jade.

鏡離臺

鑄瀉黃金鏡始開。初生三五月裴回。為遭無限塵蒙蔽。不得華堂上玉臺。

POEMS FOR HOLY PEOPLE, HOLY PLACES

On Beyond-the-Clouds Temple, I

I have heard of the moss
at Beyond-the-Clouds:

where winds blow high,
where sun is near,
it's free of the finest dust.

When level cloudbanks splash
their dye
on the Lotus Wall,

it seems to wait for a poet
and for the jewel moon.

賦凌雲寺二首

聞說凌雲寺裏苔。風高日近絕纖一作塵埃。橫雲點染芙蓉壁。似待詩人寶月來。

On Beyond-the-Clouds Temple, II

聞說凌雲寺裏花。飛空遶磴逐江斜。有時鎖得嫦娥鏡。鑠出瑤臺五色霞。

I have heard of the flowers
at Beyond-the-Clouds:

they fly through empty air,
swirl round steps of stone,
follow the river's curve.

In season, a fret of petals
edges the mirror moon,

inscribing rosy clouds
on the Moon Lady's
marble keep.

64

竹郎廟前多古木。夕陽沈沈山更綠。何處江村有笛聲。聲聲盡是迎郎一作仙曲。

題竹郎廟

Written on Lord-Bamboo Shrine

Before Lord-Bamboo Shrine:
how many ancient trees!

When sun at evening
slips away,
the hills go greener still.

From what village
by what stream
do bamboo flutes ring out?

Singing, singing: each
sound a song
welcoming the lord.

.

On Visiting the Shrine at Shamanka Mountain

Where gibbons howl
distraught and wild,
I visit Highpath Shrine.

The trail goes into sunset mists—
scents of herbs and trees.

The mountains' vivid beauty:
still
can't forget that poet.

The sound of waters:
crying yet
for King Xiang,
bereft.

Dawn after dawn
night after night
down beneath Yang Ledge,

making
clouds and making
rain,
and Chu, his kingdom, lost.

Forlorn and mournful
before the shrine:
so many willow trees

dispute the length
of their green-painted brows
in vain
when springtime comes.

調巫山廟

亂猿啼處訪高唐。路入煙霞草木香。山色未能忘宋玉。水聲猶是哭襄王。朝朝夜夜陽臺下。

為雨為雲楚國亡。惆悵廟前多少柳。春來空鬬畫眉長。

菌閣芝樓杳靄中。霞開深見玉皇宮。紫陽天上神仙客。稱在人間立世功。

寄詞

Lyric Sent to a Taoist Recluse

Mushroom towers and fungus mansions
secluded in cumuli:

when the red clouds part
look deep and see
the Jade King's celestial palace.

You, who in Purple-Yang Heaven
are the guest of gods and sylphs,

are praised here in the human realm
for deeds
to outlive this world.

Poem in Response to the Taoist Teacher Yang's "On Being Summoned to Court"

The distant streams still flow
clean and clear and pure.

Your snowy windows:
retired on high
and level with the clouds.

You don't envy the ascetic
in his fireless cell;

you merely laugh
at the Greybeard Hermits
and the worldly fame
they won.

酬楊供奉法師見招

遠水長流潔復清。雪窗高臥與雲平。不嫌袁室無煙火。惟笑商山有姓名。

許廁高齋唱。消泉定不如。可憐離記室。流水滿禪居。

宣上人見示與諸公唱和

On Being Presented to Monk Xuan: A Poem to Rhyme with Those by the Gathered Nobles

Permitted to mingle in your lofty study
I chant these words:

a seeping spring,
I cannot measure up.

Wonderful, this room,
like the learned Cleric Qiao's.

A rush of flowing waters
fills the Zen abode.

Listening to a Monk Play the Reed Pipes

聽僧吹蘆管

曉蟬鳴咽慕鴛愁。言語殷勤十指頭。罷閱梵書聊一弄。散隨金磬泥清秋。

Dawn cicadas choke back sobs.
Evening orioles grieve.

Lively language,
quick,
precise,
from ten fingers' tips.

He's done with reading holy texts.
He wants to play a bit.

His tune floats after
temple chimes
to gild clear autumn's air.

🌿 NATURE POEMS

Water Chestnut and Salad-Rush Pond

Salad-rushes
droop, meandering
where the green cress floats.

Willow floss and
mingling leaves
couch upon clear currents.

When shall we near the headwaters
and admire these things,

whirled back to pluck the chestnut blooms,
whirled back
in drifting boats?

菱荇沼

水荇斜牽綠藻浮。柳絲和葉臥清流。何時得向溪頭賞。旋摘菱花旋泛舟。

73

Lotus-Gathering Boat

採蓮舟

風前一葉壓荷蕖。解報新秋又得魚。兔走烏馳人語靜。滿溪紅袂櫂歌初。

Lotus-laden,
pushing through,
a single windblown leaf

tells the news: it's fall again,
time to fish
and sport.

The moon-hare runs, the sun-crow flies,
human chatter stills.

Pink tinted sleeves fill up the brook
and poling songs
begin.

春致風景駐仙霞。水面魚身總帶花，人世不思靈卉異。競將紅纈染輕沙。

海棠溪

Crabapple Brook

Spring sets the scene among
celestial dawn-pink clouds.

On the face of the water:
the shapes of fish,
each one trailing flowers.

Our world forgets the
otherness
of numinous green things,

while these trees compete
to dye light sands
with their rosy, dappled silk.

75

Gazing at Stonebarrel Mountain in Early Morning: Sent to Imperial Censor Lu

When the sun-cart's wheels first turn
they shine on spirits' doors.

In a whirl, they cleave
haze and mists,
ascending the deep gloom.

We point,
but never reach
that unfathomable corona.

The far horizon's murky turquoise
floods forth with blue,
clear blue.

斛石山曉望寄呂侍御

曦輪初轉照仙扃。旋摩煙嵐上窅冥。不得玄暉同指點。天涯蒼翠漫青青。

Sketch of Stonebarrel Mountain

Hills and rivers in landscape
paintings of the Wangs:

all is expressed
through appearances—
white lead powder,
ink.

But today I chanced to climb
a barren scene
and gaze

at Stepsway Ridge,
at Kingfisher Cap,
at their thousand peaks.

斛石山書事、

王家山水畫圖中。意思都盧粉墨容。今日忽登虛境望。步搖冠翠一千峯。

77

摩訶池贈蕭中丞

昔以多能佐碧油。今朝同泛舊仙舟。淒涼逝水頹波遠。惟有_{一作到}碑_泉_{一作前}咽不流。

For Vice-President Xiao of the Tribunal of Censors: On the Pond His Ancestor Made

Long ago Xiao used his talents
to shape this oil-smooth green.

And we, this morning, float
together
in an aging pleasure boat.

Chilly waters passing on:
waves tumble toward the distance.

Only the spring
in front of the monument
chokes up,
doesn't flow.

78

River-Moon Tower: Thinking of the Southland

These autumn winds are chilly,
like the cool streams
down in Wu.

Flocks of gulls and egrets
flash in evening sun.

A rainbow's arc—
embracing, damp—curves
down to the watchtower gate.

The walls' embrasures—
deep—look
out at fishing skiffs below.

When the children here in Yang'an
clap their hands
and laugh,

it makes you see this landscape
as scenery of the south.

江月樓

秋風彷彿吳江冷。鷗鷺參差夕陽影。垂虹納納臥譙門。雉堞眈眈俯漁艇。暘安小兒拍手笑。使君幻出江南景。

79

平臨雲鳥八窗秋。壯壓西川四十州。諸將莫貪羌族馬。最高層處見邊頭。

籌邊樓

For the Opening of Border Strategy Tower

Level with
the clouds and birds:
eight windows look out over fall.

Western Rivers' forty garrisons
are under firm control.

Not one general covets
the Tibetan tribes'
fine steeds.

From the tower top one sees
where
the frontier starts.

Westcliff

Lean on the rail and turn
your thoughts back
to Li Bo—riding whales!

Holding wine, you
face the wind, hand
beckoning
on its own.

Surrounded by a fine rain's patter,
I stop
the horse that takes me off:

within long rays of evening sun,
cicadas cry out,
wild.

西巖

凭闌卻憶騎鯨客。把酒臨風手自招。細雨聲中停去馬。夕陽影裏亂鳴蜩。

錦城春望

和風裝點錦城春。細雨如絲壓玉塵。漫把詩情訪奇景。艷花濃酒屬閒人。

Spring View of Chengdu, the Brocade City

Moist warm winds
dot with rouge and powder
the Brocade City's spring.

Silken threads of thin-drawn rain
press petals'
jade-white dust.

This rare scene's washed
with the urge for poems.

Glistening flowers
and unstrained wine
belong to one at ease.

🌿 POEMS ON POETRY

酬文使君

延英曉拜漢恩新。五馬驔驤九陌塵。今日謝庭飛白雪。巴歌不復醫陽春。

In Response to Lord Commissioner Wen

In Abiding Glory Palace, morning court:
the grace of Han times, renewed.

Down the capital's nine boulevards
your five steeds pranced,
raised dust.

Now, Xie's song in the garden
of that clan of poets—
you set "White Snow" to flying.

But my country ditties
can't bring back old odes,
can't bring back "Sunny Spring."

In Response to Licentiate Zhu, Thirteenth of His Generation

Your grand thoughts have the gloss
and coolness
of Blue Mountain's marbled jade

or a bag of ice
smashed to shards
on a golden plate from the south.

When master poets hone
their tools, their fame lives on.

Why bother to check
the passing list posted
on Exam Hall Gate?

酬祝十三秀才

浩思藍一作南山玉彩寒。冰囊敲碎楚金盤。詩家利器馳聲久。何用春闈榜下看。

酬杜舍人

雙魚底事到儂家。撲手新詩片片霞。唱到白蘋洲畔曲。芙蓉空老蜀江花。

In Response to Grand Secretary Du
of the Imperial Cabinet

Why has your thoughtful "paired fish" letter
come to my simple house?

Your new poems
written in a sweeping hand:
red clouds, streak on streak.

I chanted them
till I reached the song
to the tune "White Duckweed Shallows."

But this autumn flower
ages uselessly,
this
"blossom of Sichuan's streams."

87

Sending Old Poems to Yuan Zhen

The urge to make poems:
everyone's got it.

But I alone
really grasp
rich subtleties of scenes.

I sing of flowers beneath the moon,
loving what's still and pale,

or write of willows at rainy dawn
for sake of their angled fringe.

Women like Green Jade
have long been kept
hidden in secret depths.

And yet, I always write
as I please,
on my scarlet poem-slips.

Grown old, one can't collect one's work
and fix up all that's wrong,

so I send these poems to you,
as if shown to teach a boy.

寄舊詩與元微之

詩篇調態人皆有。細膩風光我獨知。月下詠花憐暗澹。雨朝題柳爲敧垂。長教碧玉藏深處。總向紅牋寫自隨。老大不能收拾得。與君開似敎男兒。

 NOTES TO THE POEMS

**Poem in Answer to Someone's "After the Rains,
Taking Pleasure among the Bamboo"**
The *yongwu* poems of Xue Tao and her peers may remind some readers of medieval and Renaissance allegorical poetry of the West. This particular poem mingles vivid description of bamboo during the spring rainy season (its rain-dampened grayish green sheen suggesting a dust of snow or frost) with references to the historical and moral associations of the giant grass.

Although the somewhat Bohemian "seven sages" of the Jin dynasty held their literary parties in bamboo groves, the plant had a prior connection with the faithful widows of the legendary Emperor Shun; their tears were said to have stained the spotted leaves of one species. The poet identifies herself here with the figure of the bamboo as self-contained (it grows by itself, not intermixed with other species), spiritually elevated ("empty heart" suggests not only the hollow stalk of the plant but Buddhist and Taoist philosophical detachment from mundane affairs), and possessing moral integrity (the bamboo is constant, remaining green all winter, and the word for the joints or nodes between the bamboo sections puns on "virtue" or "chastity"). The poem Xue is responding to is lost now, but its author seems to have been more interested in pleasure than in chastity.

Cicadas
This lowly, short-lived insect was long a figure of poverty, purity, and virtue in obscurity. In poems dating back to the Han dynasty cicadas are associated with the sorrow of autumn. Variant texts of Xue's poem read "the many leaves," "the ancient [hence, withered, dry] leaves," or "the original/ home [as in 'hometown'] leaves." My translation attempts to cover two possible readings of one line: the cicadas are said to be like the leaves and—at least in a secondary reading—to be "fasting." The early twentieth-century critic Tan Zhengbi suggests that the poem was written in self-defense against slanderous gossip about Xue Tao's relationships with male poets: the cicadas sing, but do not live, together. But this seems to limit the poem's broader comment on the human condition. The original is beautifully onomatopoeic.

Wind
The language of this poem would have reminded Xue's original audience of famous earlier poems on the wind. Its sounds echo the soughing of rustling trees.

Moon

This is a kind of riddle poem. Edward Schafer has translated *po*, the moon's "nascent crescent spirit," as "white-soul" or "protopsyche." It embodies the latent *yin* force of the moon when it is less than half-full. The full moon, on the other hand, is here said to be modeled on the disc-shaped white silk fan in a famous poem by a Han dynasty concubine, in which she evokes her purity, her beauty, and her fear of being discarded as a fan is when cool autumn arrives.

Where on earth can such a thing be seen? Nowhere, of course: the moon in its changing splendor hangs far overhead; and everywhere: its beauty is visible to us all.

Peonies

The lush, fragrant peony was tremendously popular in Tang gardens, and many poems were written about it; they often have the melancholy air of late spring. The flowers were frequently compared to beautiful women, especially courtesans like Xue Tao. Here, the deep red petals suggest the special scarlet paper used for poem exchanges between gallants and the women of the entertainment quarters, just as the drops of dew upon them suggest tears, or ink for writing love plaints. The blossoms' scent reminds one of past springs and of silent communication over distance.

The human king who shared one night of love with the goddess of Witch Gorge longed for her ever after. The original poem also alludes to the Shangri-La known as "Wuling," the lost utopia of Tao Qian's "Peach Blossom Spring"; it, too, evokes an obsession unsatisfied.

Poem Rhyming with Liu Yuxi's "Jade Rose of Sharon"

The rose of Sharon (*shun, Hibiscus syriacus*) is related to hollyhocks, mallows, and hibiscuses. As the poem's ending suggests, it was noted for the transitory beauty of its blossoms, which open in the morning and die at evening. Earlier poets had associated the flowers with the moon, dew, jade, and feminine beauty. If the poem by the famous poet and statesman Liu Yuxi (772-842), to which Xue is responding, were still extant, we might better guess just how suggestive the third stanza's reference to the flower's center was meant to be.

Seeing-Off a Friend

An old folksong in *The Book of Songs* uses the phrase "reeds and rushes" in the plaint of a woman seeking an absent lover in frosty autumn. The dusky green of the moonlit mountains brings with it associations of distance and attractiveness. The poem denies the impending separation: dreams (whether those of the woman about the traveler, or those of the traveler himself) can cover the distance between them. Yet the final simile is a reminder of just how far it is to the borderlands for which the friend is leaving.

Seeing-Off Associate Secretary Yao

The breaking off of a willow branch to be presented to a departing friend is a standard motif in Tang poetry because of the homophony of "willow" and "to stay" (or "to cause to stay"). Xue combines with this the association of the willow tree with the courtesan, perhaps in reference to her own unfaded "autumnal" beauty. The last line is beautifully ambiguous. Literally it says "don't allow mist moonlight pair towns sorrow." This can be read "Prevent the sadness of misty moonlight [seen from] two [separated] towns," or "Don't let [me, the courtesan who is represented by the hazy willow trees the poets have called] 'misty moonlight' two-town-wise sorrow [feel the sorrow of our living in two different towns]."

Seeing-Off Zheng, Prefect of Meizhou

At the end of the original poem Xue Tao mentions the famous Qin Luofu. The Han era ballad about her, "Mulberry by the Path," tells of Luofu's beauty and her steadfast loyalty to her husband. It also describes her husband in language echoed by Xue when she describes the man she is seeing off: "east," "thousand mounts," and "the column's head."

This suggests that the poem is a farewell for someone who was more to Xue than a visiting dignitary and adds interest to the question of Zheng's identity. As prefect of Meizhou he would have lived a short distance southwest of Chengdu, near "Mothbrow Mountain," Mount Emei. Xue might have accompanied him through Meizhou to Mount Emei, after which the main road turned—as the poem suggests—east to the Tuo River. The Japanese scholar Karashima Takeshi suggested that Zheng is Zheng Yin, who held a government post in Chengdu until 785 when Xue would have been in her late teens, the age of Luofu in the old ballad. The official biographies of Zheng Yin describe him as gifted and well-educated.

Gazing at Spring: Four Poems

This sequence is much anthologized, perhaps because its simple language and straighforward sentiments make the poems easy to understand. Or perhaps it is because the mask Xue Tao wears here would not jar a traditionalist notion of the aims and interests of a female poet. Certainly one reason is the lyrical melancholy of the evocative descriptions of springtime. The old association of spring with sexuality in Chinese poetry and the almost obsessive repetition of key words in Xue's original poems heighten the poignancy of the laments.

Such repetition runs counter to the usual conventions for more elevated poetry in the Tang but is common in the tradition to which the poems essentially belong, the female persona folk lyrics of the preceding era, the "Six Dynasties." There must have been a custom of tying love knots with the "love-knot herb" (literally, "same-heart grass"); they appear in other literary imitations of Six Dynasties folk poems and in a Tang dynasty list of song titles from the entertainment world.

The "one who understands my songs" in the second poem is an allusion to a famous story appearing in texts compiled in the first century B.C. There it describes grief at the death of a friend; the survivor was so distraught he broke the strings of his "zither," or *qin*, and never played again.

My version of the fourth poem in the group takes some liberty with an image drawn from the "palace plaint" tradition of courtly verse. Again and again in these poems we see the figure of a woman weeping before her mirror, her elaborate grooming made pointless by her beloved's absence. The original phrase "jade chopsticks" has been expanded in stanza three of the translation.

Homethoughts

The title of this poem suggests that it might have been written for someone from Xue's ancestral city, Chang'an. Its depth of feeling implies a real attachment. The original tells us that the river Min, flowing below "Mothbrow Mountain," looks like oil, but the connotations of the simile are more positive in Chinese, suggesting gloss and stillness.

Autumn, Hearing the Headwaters on a Moonlit Night

A more literal translation of this poem's title would be "Autumnal Spring," with "spring" meaning "the source of a creek." The opening image is that of a trail of mist rising from the water, a phenomenon of cool nights and warm days, as in the fall. This line of haze has been "clarified" (as water clears when impurities settle) by the frost-white light of the moon. The comparison of the spring's gurgling to the sound of a stringed instrument is a subtle variation on a topos dating back at least to the third century A.D., that of rising at midnight, sleepless and melancholy, to play music. Here the music is indistinct, reminding us that though the creek—or its mist—is visible, its source is far off, imagined, like the absent lover.

Riverbank

Wild geese, like the west wind, are traditionally associated with fall; they also appear in legends and poems as symbols of letters (or, more sadly, of no letters) from those far away. A Han era ballad describes a love letter written on white silk and hidden inside a fish. Here Xue Tao compares such secret love notes to Taoist talismans, the words of which magically enable the recipient to travel—at least in her dreams—to the river where her lover is.

Willow Floss

This witty poem plays on the allegorical association of the willow tree with the courtesan. The original, too, puns on "root" as "tree roots" and "fundamentally." The Chinese word rendered "light" suggests both "lightweight" and "frivolous."

Mountain Pear Blossoms: Poem Rhyming with One by Li, General of the Armies

This flattering poem turns on another stock image for the courtesan, the bush-warbler, or oriole. (This musical bird, *cettia cantans*, is not nearly as flashy as the bright yellow and black American oriole.) It seems that the courtesans are entertaining Li, who, like the talented scholar-official and calligrapher of the Liang dynasty, Wu Jun, has had flowering trees transplanted into his garden; its name, "Marsh Orchid [or Angelica] Garden," goes back even farther, at least to the Han.

Banquet Poem for Minister Wu Yuanheng, Governor of the Western Rivers District *and* Another Banquet Poem for Minister Wu

This pair of poems prettily presents the splendor of the entertainments given by Wu Yuanheng, the poet and statesman who became military governor of the Western Rivers District when Xue was in her early forties. The poems make the rhetorical gestures usual to those written on the occasion of a banquet; they also remind the reader of time's passing and of human efforts to make it stay.

The original of line one of the first poem makes use of an ambiguity in the language to describe the city walls simultaneously as "thick" and as "multiple," that is, there are ramparts within ramparts, and the evening fog is caught between them. Wu, we're told, has ordered the moon itself to light the courtyard outside the banquet hall; descriptions of rulers as having such cosmos-ordering powers are common to praise-poems in England as well as China. Xue cleverly plays on a standard poetic phrase for the crescent moon, "jade hook," suggesting that its evanescent slender bow might serve as the curtain hook that keeps the hall's gorgeous blinds rolled up so the banqueters can see outside.

The second poem focuses on the splendor of the guests, whose fur hair clasps (or hat clasps) and dragon-shaped insignia reveal their official status. Such impressive regalia were appropriate for a celebration, in early spring, of the new lunar year. Again, the poem ends on a melancholy note, however, as the long colorful horn blown by the troops at dawn and dusk signals the start of the festivities—and reminds us that the happy gathering will eventually come to an end.

Rained-Out on the Mid-Autumn Festival: Two Poems

The Mid-Autumn Festival (or "Double Yang" or "Ninth Day") falls on the ninth day of the ninth lunar month. The number nine connects it with the sunny, male *yang* principle, while its season associates it with the rising of the dark, damp, female *yin*. These two poems make use of standard features of "Ninth Day" poems and gatherings: chrysanthemums, dogwood, a climb to a hilltop. But the poet plays with them in her own way.

The first poem reminds her audience not to feel sorry about cancelled plans; human disappointments seem less important next to the brave beauty of doomed autumn flowers. The second mingles the motifs of rainy weather and sweet fragrance in the figure of the "goddess" or "water nymph" (*shennü*), one of the watery, erotic, female spirits associated with the *yin* principle. The phrase translated "good time" has, in the original, implications of a romantic encounter. Perhaps the final "clouds and rain"—a euphemism for sexual intercourse—offers the possibility of a consolation for the spoiled picnic.

A Wandering Tour of the Countryside in Spring: Sent to Master Sun *and* Another Poem for Master Sun

The informal diction of the originals of these "thank-you-note" poems and the absence of learned rhetorical flourishes tell us that the social distance between poet and recipient was not great. "Master Sun" was evidently a gentleman who had no official rank. He may have been a neighbor of Xue Tao's in her old age.

The second poem turns on a pretty conceit. The flowery fields that the party visited are compared to a kind of block-printed silk and then to embroidered sitting mats.

Sent upon Being Ill and Unable to Accompany Minister Duan on an Excursion to Wudan Temple

This work, written when the poet was in her mid- or late fifties, is an interesting variation on an outing poem. Xue sends her regrets that, due to illness, she was unable to join a party headed by military governor Duan Wenchang in visiting a temple in the northwest section of Chengdu. She wittily plays on the name of one of the sights there, a large memorial stone called "Stone Mirror." The comparison of tumbleweed to hair disheveled because of emotional distress (and, here, illness) goes back to the ancient *Book of Songs*.

Written to Thank Licentiate Yong for a Painting of the Yangzi Gorges

This poem begins with a description of the famous scenery depicted in the painting Xue Tao has been given and moves to a statement about the poet's spiritual aspirations. The original says that she wants to "pillow on streams," a malapropism from an old story in which a young man explains that using water currents for a pillow would cleanse the ears of the world's impure clamor. The last line of the translation is an addition intended to give the American reader some sense of the powerful images the name of Qutang Gorge would have evoked for Xue's primary audience.

Written to Thank Auxiliary Xin for a Spray of Flowers

The poet enriched this simple "thank-you" by drawing on a trove of mythic imagery. A "blue-black bird" is often a messenger of the immortals, especially of the divine Western Queen Mother who dwells in the remote, numinous Kunlun range of Central Asia. The branch seems to become a spray from the jeweled world-tree that grows there. When Xue describes her own home as "a terrace of moon-bright jade" (*yaotai*), she associates it with the dwelling of the lovely, lonely goddess Chang'e on the moon.

Trying on New-Made Clothes: Three Poems

This set of "thank-you" poems uses elaborate Taoist celestial imagery, a common convention of Tang verse written for high-ranking government figures. The first poem equates the heavenly Purple-Yang Palace with the residence of whoever gave the clothing to the poet. It then compares the dark red raw silk to the lovely mists of the faraway faerie islands in the eastern sea. A second length of fabric—this one ice-white—is said to be as cool as the fur of the rabbit who lives in the moon. It has wondrous origins: the giant "ice-silkworms" lived in frost and snow on a magic mountain. Chang'e, the moon goddess, confirms the other-worldly origin of the cloth by pointing to the bridge (in the original) used by the Weaver Woman Star, Vega, in her annual tryst with her lover.

In the second poem the making and decorating of the material is imagined in similar supernatural detail. The "Nine Humors" (*jiuqi*), the variegated clouds of sunrise (or sunset), and the "Five Magic Beasts" all suggest that magical energy has been woven into a pink or multicolor textile of ethereal beauty called "Five Cloud" cloth. Extravagant fabrics with images of divine animals were evidently available in Xue's day, so the pattern of the cloth might have included the Five Magic Beasts—tortoise, dragon, a kind of unicorn (*qilin*), white tiger, and the so-called phoenix (*fenghuang*)—as well as the flowers whose prototypes belong to the East Lord, god of the spring.

The last poem of the set describes the finished clothing and the setting in which it is worn. The garments are said to have been presented originally in one of the three Taoist heavenly realms. Those attendant on the giver of the cloth are here transformed into immortals holding ceremonial scepters shaped like a fungus prized by Taoist adepts. The song they sing was intoned by initiates in a ritual dance.

For Someone Far Away: Two Poems

The view of poetry as having the capacity and the obligation for moral commentary on human affairs is an old one in China. These two poems draw on the tradition of female persona poetry to make their statement against war and its attendant sorrows, in a mingling of the personal and the objective. It is not necessary to assume that Xue Tao in fact had a lover at the front;

95

Chinese poems protesting war often focused on those left behind. But her patron Wei Gao's military expeditions, for example, suggest that she might have written this poem with someone specific in mind.

The autumn-blooming "his-face-flowers" (this name was used for both a kind of lotus, *Nelumbo nucifera*, and a member of the hibiscus family) were traditionally used as a pun on "his face [that is, the face of the man I love]." "A lover's letter" is, literally, "embroidered words," an allusion to the story of a third-century B.C. woman who embroidered a sequence of palindromic poems and sent the cloth to her husband, a general who was away on duty. The end of the first poem draws on the familiar figure of the woman awaiting the return of her beloved as the speaker climbs to the top of a building called, in the original, the "Gazing-After-Him Tower."

The second poem contrasts the potential fecundity of the willows—as elsewhere suggesting women, especially courtesans—with a striking image of blockage. The lovers' springtime, their youth and sexuality, is being wasted.

On Being Banished to the Borderlands: Submitted to Commander Wei *and* Another Poem for Commander Wei on Being Banished

Poems set in the Tang empire's harsh frontier lands in Central Asia are among the greatest of the age. Not everyone who wrote them actually went there, but it seems probable that Xue really was banished for a time. The many textual variants in the originals of these poems indicate that they circulated widely.

The best evidence suggests that these poems were written for Xue Tao's patron, Wei Gao. However, the later military governor Wu Yuanheng is named as the recipient in one text. Another source tells us that the mutinous general Liu Pi banished Xue, and it has also been suggested that the poems were sent to the poet Yuan Zhen en route to her place of punishment. (Did Xue refuse to serve the upstart Liu during his brief tenure as de facto governor in Chengdu?) And finally, there is a persistent—but anachronistic—tradition that the poems were written for Gao Pien, a *late* ninth-century military governor; this might mean that the poems were actually occasioned by a banishment by Gao Pien's grandfather, the general Gao Chongwen, who defeated Liu Pi and brought Chengdu back into the imperial fold. (Perhaps Xue Tao collaborated with Liu after all and suffered the consequences. She did write an extravagant poem of praise for Gao Chongwen, not translated in this collection.) The two banishment poems following this pair are said to have been addressed to either Wu Yuanheng or Gao Chongwen. If all four are indeed autobiographical, and if Xue Tao was not banished twice, then the case for Wu or Gao as recipient of these two poems is strengthened.

The first poem subtly depicts the inappropriateness and pathos of the banishment by juxtaposing the *artiste*'s elegant melody with her new audience, the unrefined troopers and hicks of the northwest frontier. This is a nice variation on the "barbarian" (Central Asian) music that is part of the standard furniture of border poems.

The second poem begins with a derogatory term for the enemy against whom the garrisons were maintained. The Tibetans in their obstinate perversity steadfastly continue to deviate from the commands of the Son of Heaven. In contrast, the speaker is dutiful, submitting to the punishment of her overlord with good grace. Songzhou was the northernmost prefectural city of Shu. "The road home from" is my interpolation; the speaker may have been sent only as far away as Songzhou, at the southern edge of the Longtou mountains, or the town may have represented the first sign of home on the return route south from farther away.

On Arriving at the Borderlands: Submitted to Minister Wu *and* Another Poem for Minister Wu on Arriving at the Borderlands

The first of these poems simultaneously evokes the atmosphere of the steppes and establishes a flattering allegory for the poet's relationship to the man the poem was written for. The bright moon that appears in so many frontier poems is also the human luminary from whom she is now so far removed. The tiny firefly suggests both her relative insignificance and the sparse grasses of the northwest in which the insects hover (and from which tradition said they were born). The original plays on the word *xin*, "letters," which also means "sincerity" or "loyalty."

The second poem begins with another pun: the opening phrase, literally, "check the rains at the top of the ridge," seems also to be a place name. The ironically described cold of the place leads the poet to declare that, should she receive amnesty and return to her humble dwelling in Chengdu, she will never again look at mountainous terrain, not even in paintings on decorative screens.

Dog Parted from Her Master

This is the first of Xue's famous "Ten Partings" sequence, which was probably written after a falling out with her friend and lover, the poet Yuan Zhen, though it may have been written for her patron, governor Wei Gao. The clever puns on amatory language encouraged a wide circulation for the poems; consequently, there are a number of textual variants.

"Crimson gates" suggests a mansion. "Took a nip" is my own insertion; it is intended to replace other double meanings lost in translation. One explanation for the composition of the sequence is that Xue had angered the recipient by throwing a wine pot and hurting a guest—perhaps when she was tipsy.

97

Writing Brush Parted from the Hand

A comparison of herself to a writing brush was certainly appropriate for a skilled calligrapher like Xue Tao. It also shows how quickly this sequence of poems leaves behind the humility of her first allegory for herself, the dog. The brush described here is made of high-quality materials: bamboo from the far southeast and fur from what is now Jiangxi province. The gemstones and flowers it scatters on red slips of paper (red was especially used for poems sent by gallants to courtesans) suggest both the ornamental images of love poetry and the beautiful appearance of calligraphy on the page. Wang Xizhi was the master calligrapher of the Six Dynasties period in whose style Xue herself was said to have written so well. The images and language of the original are teasingly suggestive.

Horse Parted from Her Stable

"Young master jadeface" is presumably the person who was hit by the wine pot Xue Tao threw, thus offending Yuan Zhen, if that story of the poems' origin is true; "jade" suggests he had both purity of character and personal beauty. The chariot (more literally, "flowery cart") is an ornate carriage such as belonged to high-ranking officials. Yet lauditory though all this is, it is subtly overshadowed by the dazzling appearance and supernatural swiftness of the horse, who reminds the reader of other mythic Chinese horses in her ability to race beyond the horizons where the sun rises and sets.

Parrot Parted from Her Cage

Parrots and parakeets were popular pets in well-to-do households of Tang China. They were valued—like the courtesans to whom they were often compared—for their bright beauty and their verbal skill. But of course it was these very qualities that caused them to be caged.

This bird came from the Long Mountains in the wild lands north of Chengdu, along the modern Shenxi-Gansu border. My "desert wastes" replaces the original's "west of the Long"; the name of this arid district puns on the word for cage, hence the replacement pun in my final line, "deserted cage." Similarly, "to call out" is a traditional pun on "to enjoy, to make joyful," and "brocade" suggests Chengdu, the Brocade City.

Swallow Parted from Her Nest

In this next metamorphosis the poet becomes a swallow; "lovebird" or "turtledove" might be an appropriate Western equivalent. The free translation "mate-sweet-mate" renders an equally onomatopoeic birdcall from the ancient *Book of Songs*. Swallows' nests in the rafters were a sign of coming good fortune; the fragile nests have also been used to suggest insecure positions. A coral pillow implied official promotion and longevity for its owner.

Pearl Parted from the Palm

In Tang times pearls were seen as tiny moons. This one, we're told, reflects light from the crystal palace located on the moon. Many of these poems subtly warn the recipient that he has lost something valuable in sending the poet away; here the traditional symbolic relationship between pearls and women is used to make that point.

Fish Parted from the Pond

This poem is especially rich in erotic wordplay—and in textual variants. The word "fish" is a common pun for "desire," and fish sporting amorously among lotuses, as this one did, appear in many ballads and poems from at least Han times on. "Deep lovely" renders both of two varying texts' modifiers for "pond": "deep" may have sexual overtones in some contexts, and the other version's original "lotus" was a stock pun for "love" (hence my "lovely" rather than the literal flower).

"The silky line" (literally, "fishline-silk") also puns on both "love" and "love-longing." A textual variant in this line replaces "fishline-silk" with "silver." "Silver hooks" was a standard description for elegant calligraphy, but the phrase may play here on the similar-sounding yin ("shady, genital") hook; certainly "hook" seems to have been used as an appellation for "penis" in other amatory poems. This is supported by the context: "his-face-lily" evokes a lover, and "clear" (qing) resonates as the aurally and visually similar "sentiment, passion."

Though the translation uses the pronoun "she," the original has none. As in the last two poems in the sequence, then, the ending might be read as a far less repentant "you are no longer going to get to. . . ."

Falcon Parted from the Gauntlet

Hawking was popular among those in medieval China who could afford it. This falcon, with her eyes like bells, is capable, untamed, a strong and unrepentant figure. "Noble, lofty cloud" (literally, "pale-gray cloud," qing yun) is a standard expression of praise; it refers not only to the actual clear sky but to a person of extraordinary learning and scholary reputation or elevated official rank. Thus the poet compliments the poem's recipient, while pointing out that this bird has flown.

Bamboo Parted from the Pavillion

As in the first poem of this collection, Xue reminds us of the bamboo's allegorical representation of moral strength and sexual chastity. But at the same time she uses the traditional association of springtime with sexual desire: those bamboo shoots that so vigorously penetrated the pavillion wall are "springtime shoots." And though the images of the last words ostensibly refer to the shade of leaves and a high-class dwelling (of which the pavillion is a part), the language suggests possible double entendres.

Mirror Parted from Its Stand

Old Chinese mirrors were round, made of metal, and often kept on a little stand or "ledge." The lunar imagery here suits such a shining disk; the original says "moon paces back and forth," evoking a bright circle, quivering and arrested. The dust that covers the mirror is a common locution for slander.

Connubial images of *yin* and *yang* were frequently decorative motifs for Tang mirrors. The last line's "ledge of jade" certainly refers to an elegant mirror-stand and as a proper noun flatteringly identifies the residence of the man with whom Xue has quarreled as the celestial palace of the chief Taoist deity, the Jade Emperor himself. But the context of erotic teasing established earlier in the poem cycle suggests a subtext in which "ledge of jade" has its sexual slang meaning of "clitoris" or *mons veneris*. "Bower" (literally, "flowery hall") may have similar connotations.

On Beyond-the-Clouds Temple: Two Poems

Visiting a Buddhist temple was a favorite poetic subject for Tang poets. Descriptions of scenery tended toward the sublime or, as here, the ethereal. This temple, whose very name suggests the transmundane, was located on Beyond-the-Clouds Mountain, south of Chengdu, at the confluence of three rivers and just east of Mount Emei. The beauty of the temple and its surroundings attracted the attention of many poets, but Xue Tao had particular reason to take note of it. Early in her tenure as military governor, her patron Wei Gao ordered the restoration of a giant statue of the Maitreya Buddha at the base of the mountain; the statue may still be seen today.

The dust in the first poem and the empty air (*kong*, often translated "sky" or "void") in the second have Buddhist philosophical connotations of, respectively, the delusional realm of human activity and the emptiness that is ultimate reality. Both poems close with optical illusions that involve the overlaying of color, with its sensuous appeal, on something pure. Sun-reddened clouds cast their hues on a temple wall surrounding a lotus pond or decorated with lotuses, a common Buddhist motif. Then the round "mirror" of Chang'e, the moon goddess, is seen through pink petals that are transformed into a fretwork of rosy clouds against the background of her jade-white palace on the moon.

Written on Lord-Bamboo Shrine

This poem evokes the shrine of three apotheosized chieftains of a culture once located in what is now southwest China, south of Chengdu on the far side of the Yangzi River. This area was not under Chinese suzerainty in Xue Tao's time. The cult may have spread northward, in which case the title could mean that the poet literally wrote this poem *on* a wall of a shrine, as was not uncommon. Or she may have been describing a place she had only heard of—perhaps from one of the Chengdu youths enslaved by the invading Nanzhao in 829 and later returned. The poem's somewhat melancholy air does suggest that it is a lament for those captured and taken south, perhaps never to be greeted by their friends and relatives again. The last words of the original are richly musical with repetition and consonance. "Welcoming the Lord" is probably the title of a song associated with the cult.

On Visiting the Shrine at Shamanka Mountain

Wu Shan ("Enchantress," "Shamanka," or "Witch" Mountain) is one of the sheer peaks that form the famous Yangzi River gorges. The site has been the focus of a popular poetic subject since at least the Han era: the manifestation of a goddess of fertility and moisture to King Xiang of Chu as he lay dreaming on the mountain, their night of passionate love, and his longing for her after her departure in the morning. Xue's skillful use of alliteration, assonance, and internal rhyme suggests the eerie wail of the gibbons inhabiting the region around Highpath Shrine, a sound long associated with the melancholy of King Xiang, just as the colored mists and sweet fragrance evoke his divine lover.

"That poet" is, in the original, Song Yu (circa third century B.C.); the long poems (*fu*) that Xue Tao and other writers on this topic allude to are traditionally attributed to him. Three of the phrases Xue uses here were (because of their appearance in the two Song Yu poems or their prose introductions) euphemisms for sexual intercourse: "Highpath," "Yang Terrace/Ledge," and "clouds and rain." The spring-green willows at the end of the poem suggest human women, perhaps Xue herself, responding to the sad yet sensuous, strongly feminine, atmosphere of the place. The reference to eyebrows would have been immediately clear to readers in her time, who knew that women's long slender eyebrows, fashionably made up in greenish-black, were often compared to willow leaves.

Lyric Sent to a Taoist Recluse

The title of the original says simply "Lyric, Sent Off," but the imagery makes it clear that it was sent to a Taoist adept. The fantastic sky-castle in this poem is as beautiful and as charged with spiritual power as the various fungi used in certain Taoist elixirs. The "Jade King" (or Jade Emperor) is the supreme deity of folk Taoism.

Poem in Response to the Taoist Teacher Yang's "On Being Summoned to Court"

The Taoist "Teacher of the Law" that Xue addresses here had evidently received a summons to perform religious ceremonies in the capital and had written a poem making the usual expression of desire to remain in seclusion. The imagery of the poem's first half suggests the purity and spiritual elevation of the life in the mountains that Yang had been called away from.

A phrase in the original, "cold and lonely cell," alludes to a Han dynasty ascetic, Yuan Hong, who lived for eighteen years in a clay cell with no door and no cooking fire, intoning holy texts and unaffected even by a rebellion. But Yang, Xue states, is free of any need to indulge in competitive austerities. A similar removal from political involvement was displayed by the hermits known as "the Four Greybeards of Mount Shang," who remained in retreat from political turmoil even when summoned by the first Han emperor. They did finally go, however, becoming useful advisors to the crown prince and acquiring worldly reputations that Yang is politely depicted as distaining.

On Being Presented to Monk Xuan: A Poem to Rhyme with Those by the Gathered Nobles

The literarily inclined Buddhist monk to whom this next poem is addressed lived in Xue's region but was called away to serve in the capital when the poet was in her forties. This poem was probably written sometime before then, on some occasion when Xue joined a gathering of writers at Xuan's residence. The monk's study, and by implication he himself, are described as elevated in both location and spirit. He is compared to a third-century A.D. Sichuanese scholar, astronomer, and calligrapher, Qiao Zhou, famed for his detachment from worldly affairs.

Listening to a Monk Play the Reed Pipes

This beautifully musical poem takes on the special problem of music played by a Buddhist monk. Strictly speaking, from the Buddhist standpoint such an attractive, emotionally stirring art form ought to be shunned: it fosters attachment to the world of illusion. Yet a plaintive or ethereal melody can mingle an austere awareness with its appeal to the senses.

The opening images remind the reader of the melancholy associations of reed pipes, which came to China from the north. Though the poem moves to a less lugubrious metaphor, comparing the melody to the rise and fall of human speech, the final image points out the tension between attachment and nonattachment in this Buddhist music. The metal chimes that were struck to mark the sections of the day have autumnal and transcendent associations of long standing. Their notes, and those of the pipes, are depicted as scattering through the sky like precious gold leaf applied to a mandala or a copy of a sutra. But "to gild" (ni) also implies "to muddy."

Water Chestnut and Salad-Rush Pond

The renditions of some of the plant names here have been quite free. "Salad-rush" is actually an edible plant called xing (nymphoides pettalum), and "cress" is zao, an aquatic plant much larger than our watercress.

"Willow floss" may pun on "thoughts of remaining." "Couch" and "clear currents" are language often found in the poetry of reclusion. "The headwaters" may allude to the famous poem and preface by Tao Qian on the agrarian utopia found (and lost) at the source of Peach Blossom Stream.

Lotus-Gathering Boat

Xue Tao describes this scene in terms that mingle the human world with the green realm of plants. The pink or red sleeves suggest both women in appealing clothing and the rosy petals of the blossoms on the stream. The single leaf blown before the wind is, of course, the lotus gatherers' skiff. The original describes the boat with an ambiguous phrase; it is simultaneously presented as "weighed down by" gathered lotuses and as pushing its way through others yet unplucked.

The amatory air of many poems on this topic invites us to read Xue's with the old association of fishing and sexuality in mind. And the movements of the mythic rabbit in the moon and the three-legged sun-crow remind us of time's passing.

Crabapple Brook

There are two streams in Sichuan called "Crabapple Brook"; the better known of these is just south of the Yangzi, near modern Chungking. The transcendant rosy clouds of sunrise (or sunset) in the opening image are blooming crabapple trees, a sight associated with the region.

The poem presents other illusions. Staring at the surface of the water, one seems to see the fish below gliding upon that plane, sashed with pink silk that is actually fallen petals floating on the brook—or are they just reflected? Or is this all a fancy seen in the foam and ripples of the flowing water? The phrase that stresses the spiritual power of the natural world, here rendered "numinous green things," comes from the ancient *Book of Songs*.

Gazing at Stonebarrel Mountain in Early Morning:
Sent to Imperial Censor Lu

Stonebarrel Mountain is just north of Chengdu. The "sun-cart" is the chariot of Xihe, who drives the sun on its daily journey across the sky. The "unfathomable [or occult or arcane] corona" is the sun itself. Because the names of colors used in the final image do not correspond exactly with those of English, the poem might be taken as describing the distance-grayed greenery of the horizon turning luxuriantly green as it is overspread with light. But it more probably depicts the changes in the sky itself.

Sketch of Stonebarrel Mountain

"Hills [or mountains] and rivers" is the Chinese idiom for "landscape." In the original, as in the translation, the reader is a few words into the poem before learning whether a painting or the earth itself is being described. The poet continues to play with the concept of illusion, reminding us that paintings (and therefore, all that they manage to express or even to create) are entirely effects of the artist's paint and powdered pigment.

Similarly the phrase "barren scene" has been used not only to describe a desolate, hilly territory but as a Buddhist term for "the realm free of passions." The implication here is that the scene viewed from the hilltop was both a wasteland and a reminder of the reality behind the apparently real, the Void. The poem closes with one more reversal. Just as a flat painting in black and white re-presents a three-dimensional scene, so when the poet climbed to this empty place she suddenly saw the manifold peaks of nearby mountains whose very names suggest life, color, and the allure of human appearances.

For Vice-President Xiao of the Tribunal of Censors: On the Pond His Ancestor Made

A sixth-century figure named Xiao Mohe is said to have constructed Mohe Pond (evidently by damming a stream) in the western part of Chengdu. "Oil-smooth green" (more literally, "jade-green oil") suggests not only the appearance of the water but also a green, rain-repellent canopy used by important military men. Since the word rendered "shape" also means "to aid, assist," it seems the poet has managed to pay tribute to the elder Xiao while commending her contemporary of the same surname for his work as an assistant in the military government of Chengdu. At the same time, the old boat, the water departing for the sea, the stagnating pond, and the memorial stele remind us of the passing away of all things.

River-Moon Tower: Thinking of the Southland

This poem differs in form from the rest of Xue's extant works: its six lines and the absence of tonal regulation mark it as "old-style verse," *gu shi*. It appears to have circulated separately from most of the others.

The River-Moon Tower in the title was located in Yang'an commandery, some fifty to sixty kilometers east and slightly south of Chengdu. "Wu" is an old name for the region south of the central and lower Yangzi River; much the same area—the central Yangzi Valley—is referred to in the last line by a contemporary name, "Jiangnan" (literally, "south of the Yangzi").

The poem creates an ambiance of special perspective afforded by the tower. From its top one can see what the original text calls a "hanging rainbow" (perhaps a curved, painted bridge) arching over to the watchtower. The tower allows the poem's addressee (perhaps fictive, but called by the respectful second person pronoun *jun*, "milord") to view this pleasant scene and to make the imaginative leap to the exotic and beautiful landscapes downstream and to the south.

For the Opening of Border Strategy Tower

This tower was built in western Chengdu as part of a general shoring-up of Tang defenses late in Xue Tao's lifetime. On its walls were charts indicating the military preparedness, civilian population, and availability of logistical support for the Chinese areas adjoining those of the non-Han peoples to the south and west. This "War Room" was probably completed in the fall of 831, but the season is also appropriate to the poem because of its martial associations.

The poet praises the Pax Sinica maintained by the border garrisons of the Jiannan "circuit" (province) Western Rivers district. And by praising, she exhorts the Chinese military leaders to restrain their desire for the excellent horses available to those who collaborated with the enemy tribal peoples in the Tibetan cultural sphere to the west.

Westcliff

The scenic location of this poem is probably southeast of Chengdu, near the River-Moon Tower. Like many of these poems, the original version has no pronouns; one possibility is that the poet, leaving Westcliff, stops for a moment to savor a late-day mixture of sunlight and drizzle when the hand of someone (here "you") come to see her off waves in the wind as if summoning her back.

The great poet Li Bo (Li Po) was sometimes called by the extravagant title "the traveler who rode a whale." Even more suggestive of escape from the mundane sphere is a variant phrase in the version of this poem handed down in the local history of the area around Westcliff, "turn your thoughts back and, riding clouds, ascend."

Spring View of Chengdu, the Brocade City

This poem may be the work of a contemporary of Xue's, a Taoist gentlewoman from Chengdu named Zhuo Yingying, but it is attributed to Xue Tao in the 1872 gazetteer for Chengdu County. The text literally describes the spring breezes as "applying makeup" to Chengdu, causing pink and white blossoms to open on the city's trees. "Jade-white dust" is poetic diction both for scattered flower petals and for snow, especially the light powder of early spring.

In Response to Lord Commissioner Wen

Tang poets often identified contemporary sites and events with the lost glories of the Han. Here Xue states that some official act of the Tang emperor in the palace where he held morning audience has revived the benevolence of bygone days; presumably this was the appointment of Wen to his present position.

The second half of the poem looks to the literary past. Xue Tao and Lord Wen are evidently at the residence of someone bearing the famous family name Xie. Snow was associated with the talented Xie clan both through the fifth-century literatus Xie Huilian's "Snow Rhapsody" (*Xue fu*) and through a famous anecdote about the fourth-century literata Xie Daoyun. In addition, "White Snow" is—like "Sunny Spring"—the name of an ancient melody for the zitherlike *qin*. These pieces were considered elevated and difficult to harmonize with and were conventionally contrasted with the rustic tunes of eastern Sichuan. Moreover, it seems that the poet cleverly uses the song titles and their associations to complain flirtatiously of a coolness in Wen's attitude toward her.

In Response to Licentiate Zhu, Thirteenth of His Generation

Here Xue values poetic skill over the scholarly achievement that could open the way to a high-status job in government service. Its recipient was a "licentiate" or *xiucai*, one who had passed the prefectural-level civil service examination; it may have been written to console him for failure in the next-level competition. The title tells us that he was the thirteenth-born in a generation of brothers and paternal first cousins. Blue (or Bluefield) Mountain was located just south of the imperial capital. Its "jade" (actually a green and white marble) and the crystalline bits of ice on a gleaming plate from the ancient southern region called Chu suggest a poetic sensibility of dazzling splendor: an older contemporary of Xue's compared the scenes evoked in poetry to the elusive sunlit mists rising off the marble of Blue Mountain.

In Response to Grand Secretary Du of the Imperial Cabinet

This poem was apparently sent to Du Yuanying, a man of considerable literary ability who later became military governor in Chengdu at the apogee of a rapid political rise and fall. If so, it can probably be dated to 820 or 821, when the poet was in her early fifties. Evidently Du had sent Xue a letter expressing concern for her and enclosing some of his poems, including one that praised her as the "blossom of Sichuan's streams." The opening question uses a conventional expression of self-deprecating surprise and with the phrase "paired fish" alludes to an old folksong about the receipt of a pair of carp from afar that contained hidden within them a letter of tender regard. The old melody "White Duckweed Shallows [or Riverbank]" may have had some special appropriateness for an exchange of correspondence between poets; since white duckweed blooms in summer and fall, it would have been an apt complimentary simile for the middle-aged Xue.

Sending Old Poems to Yuan Zhen

This poem seems to be a statement both playful and serious of Xue Tao's views on her own work, although some editors state that it was written by

Yuan Zhen *for* Xue Tao. Xue asserts here her own unique understanding of the source or material of literary art: physical scenery and human personalities. (The original of "rich subtleties of scenes" refers broadly to human character as well as landscapes.) Her writing, she tells us, grows out of the emotional responses of a refined sensibility to evocative natural objects.

The dutifully self-effacing model woman of Confucian tradition is referred to by "Green Jade." There were two famous concubines of this name: one was celebrated for her unassuming ways and awareness of her lowly place in society; the other was driven by her master to suicide in the name of chastity. Xue's rejection of these models is clear.

The conclusion shows a modesty that balances this self-assertiveness. The poet declares that she is too old to repair her work successfully and, perhaps, warns the younger poet to avoid bad writing habits while he still can. Some have read the "boy" (or "son") of the last line as evidence that Xue bore a child to Yuan.

The Man I Pretend to Be: "The Colloquies" and Selected Poems of Guido Goz-zano, translated and edited by Michael Palma, with an introductory essay by Eugenio Montale. (Italy)

D'Après Tout: Poems by Jean Follain, translated by Heather McHugh. (France)

Songs of Something Else: Selected Poems of Gunnar Ekelöf, translated by Leonard Nathan and James Larson. (Sweden)

The Little Treasury of One Hundred People, One Poem Each, compiled by Fujiwara No Sadaie and translated by Tom Galt. (Japan)

The Ellipse: Selected Poems of Leonardo Sinisgalli, translated by W. S. Di Piero. (Italy)

The Difficult Days by Roberto Sosa, translated by Jim Lindsey. (Honduras)

Hymns and Fragments by Friedrich Hölderlin, translated and introduced by Richard Sieburth. (Germany)

The Silence Afterwards: Selected Poems of Rolf Jacobsen, translated and edited by Roger Greenwald. (Norway)

Rilke: Between Roots, selected poems rendered from the German by Rika Lesser. (Germany)

In the Storm of Roses: Selected Poems by Ingeborg Bachmann, translated, edited, and introduced by Mark Anderson. (Austria)

Birds and Other Relations: Selected Poetry of Dezső Tandori, translated by Bruce Berlind. (Hungary)

Brocade River Poems: Selected Works of the Tang Dynasty Courtesan Xue Tao, translated and introduced by Jeanne Larsen. (China)

Library of Congress Cataloging-in-Publication Data

Hsüeh, T'ao, 768-831.
Brocade River poems.

(The Lockert Library of poetry in translation)
1. Hsüeh, T'ao, 768-831—Translations, English. I. Larsen, Jeanne.
II. Title.   III. Series.

PL2677.H76A24 1987   895.1'13   86-25340
ISBN 0-691-06686-8 (alk. paper)   ISBN 0-691-01434-5 (pbk.)

Milton Keynes UK
Ingram Content Group UK Ltd.
UKHW011949151223
434462UK00001B/69